A COLORSLIDE

The Pitti

FILIPPO ROSSI

32 MASTERPIECES

TOUR OF

Palace

FLORENCE

OF PAINTING VISITED WITH

FILIPPO ROSSI, ADMINISTRATOR

On the end papers:
The Room of Mars

THIS BOOK HAS BEEN PREPARED UNDER THE
SUPERVISION OF HARRY N. ABRAMS, INC.

COLORSLIDE INDEX

Your guide for this Colorslide Tour

FILIPPO ROSSI

Administrator of the Museums of the

Provinces of Florence, Arezzo, and Pistoia

As administrator of all the museums and galleries of three provinces of ancient Tuscany, Dr. Rossi has the unique honor of supervising two of the world's greatest treasure houses of art—the Uffizi and the Pitti, both in Florence. His distinguished career in art began in 1914, when he received his doctorate at the University of Florence. Thereafter, he became Director of the Museo Nazionale, the Museo di San Marco, and the Museo degli Argenti in Florence. In 1941 he was appointed administrator of all the galleries and museums of Florence; and he has held his present post since 1952.

In addition to making important contributions to the literature on Italian art—especially in the fields of sculpture, goldsmith work, and the jeweled arts—Dr. Rossi has been outstanding among leading museum men for his contributions to museum practice. These have mostly been in the direction of bringing the world's greatest art to an ever-widening public. Art lovers are greatly in his debt for his successful efforts to maintain works of art in the best possible condition and to present them to the public in the most attractive surroundings.

Hardly anyone is so well qualified as Dr. Rossi to conduct you on your tour of 32 of the masterpieces of the great Pitti Palace in Florence.

THE STORY OF
The Pitti Palace

To supplement the paintings visited on the tour, these introductory pages show important works of art from other departments in the great collections of the Pitti Palace.

A VISIT to the Pitti Palace in Florence can be one of the truly wonderful experiences in anyone's life. I will try as best I can to bring this experience to you through this Colorslide tour. Long ago, the Pitti was the palatial residence of the grand dukes of the Medici family, who ruled Florence officially during her period of decline just as their untitled ancestors had ruled the city unofficially during her period of greatness.

For two centuries—the fourteenth and fifteenth—this marvelous city was the capital of the world, the center of one of mankind's greatest adventures, the Italian Renaissance. It was a time of tremendous development in art, learning, and science. The artists and scholars of Florence tore down the walls that hemmed in the narrow world of the Middle Ages, creating a new civilization with vastly broadened horizons. The fabulously wealthy Medici banking family—most notably Cosimo de' Medici the elder and his grandson Lorenzo the Magnificent—were leaders in this rebirth of culture. They were despots, if you will, but they lavished fortunes on the beautification of their city and in support of the intellectual life. The churches of Florence and their own palaces and villas sparkled with masterpieces of painting and sculpture that they commissioned. They bought Italian art, Flemish art, and the Classical statuary newly excavated in Rome. Their collections still form the basis for Florence's two great galleries—the Pitti and the Uffizi.

VENUS
by Canova
Italian, 1757-1822

MOSAIC IN RELIEF OF GRAND DUKE
COSIMO II DE' MEDICI IN PRAYER
by Orazio Mochi
Florentine, died 1625

In the sixteenth century the Medici became the absolute rulers of Florence, assuming the grand-ducal title. But Florentine political power had waned, and her supremacy in the arts soon disappeared, snuffed out by the same breath that had fanned it into white-hot brilliance. Yet even today the presence of that ancient brilliance is everywhere, and it is a rare visitor who can move through Florence without a sense of reverence and awe.

It is with the setting of the Pitti that our tour begins—and we should imagine ourselves to be on the side of a gently sloping hill south of the river Arno. On the other side of the river we can see the city, which is clustered about the landmarks of the Cathedral, the Baptistery, Giotto's Tower, and the Palazzo Vecchio. Savonarola preached in that cathedral and burned the Vanities in that square; those streets were traveled by Dante, Boccaccio, Leonardo da Vinci, and Michelangelo.

It is more residential where we are, on the south bank of the river. Let us imagine that we are standing in the grounds behind the Pitti Palace itself, in the Boboli Gardens—one of the most important and famous parks in Italy. Here the Medici found rest and refreshment during the heat of the summer. Today, you and I may do the same, because the Gardens, like the Palace, now belong to the Italian people and are open to all.

The Boboli is a splendid example of Italian garden art. Its space is divided into large areas in which streams of water rise; these streams are used as decorative elements and feed the large number of graceful fountains.

Grottoes, seats, columns and statues, walks, tree-shaded avenues, and a lake with an island form a harmonious background to the play of water. Cleverly tying the Palace to the Gardens is the so-called Artichoke Fountain, set at the open end of the Palace court. Before this elaborate fountain, at the edge of the huge park, is the open-air amphitheater where the Medici and their court once enjoyed dramatic entertainment. In its center is a great obelisk—over 3500 years old—brought over from Thebes, in Egypt.

All the reigning Medici from the mid-sixteenth century to the eighteenth made their home in the Pitti Palace. It was bought for Eleonora of Toledo, the Spanish wife of Cosimo I de' Medici, who was the last Duke of the Republic of Florence and became the first Grand Duke of Tuscany. At first, Cosimo and Eleonora established their grand-ducal court and living apartments in the ancient Palazzo Vecchio in the center of the city. However, Eleonora had five children in the first nine years of her marriage, and found the location of the old building and the smallness of her living quarters more than she could bear. In 1549 Cosimo I bought the unfinished palace begun a century before for Luca Pitti, a great enemy of the Medici family. Pitti had been anxious that his new residence, the most ambitious of its day, be imposing in form and built of splendid materials. He engaged Brunelleschi, the great Renaissance architect, to design it in the rugged, majestic style of the fifteenth century in Florence, but never had the funds to bring it to completion. The Palace did not then have its present imposing size. Cosimo

ROCK CRYSTAL COFFRET *by Valerio Belli, Venetian, 1468-1546*

engaged the architect Ammanati to enlarge it, and the landscape architect Tribolo to design proper grounds. Ammanati built the two great wings, thereby creating the courtyard. Other Grand Dukes in the seventeenth and eighteenth centuries continued to enlarge the Palace and Boboli Gardens, until the Pitti that we know today took final shape. It is astonishing that so many architects over so long a time succeeded in harmonizing their own architectural ideas with the power and boldness of Brunelleschi's original masterpiece.

The Gallery of the Pitti occupies the entire west wing of the ground floor. It is very different in appearance from the modern type of museum gallery. In today's galleries, works of art are given restful backgrounds and plenty of room to breathe, and they are arranged in some kind of logical order; this is very helpful to the museumgoer and certainly makes art easy to see. The Pitti, however, still has its ancient character: the collection is arranged as magnificent decoration of magnificent rooms intended to give the impression of tremendous wealth and splendor. The pictures are in rich frames that cover the walls beneath gilded and frescoed ceilings. But such an

MARBLE FOUNTAIN
from the Medici Villa at Castello
STATUE
by Il Tribolo
Florentine, 1485-1550

arrangement is precious to us if we understand that the Pitti is, perhaps, the only princely Baroque gallery that is almost exactly the same today as it was when built. If the pictures are a little hard to look at, we are still given the privilege of viewing a unique aesthetic whole—the gallery itself.

The gallery assumed its present extent and appearance in the seventeenth century under the Grand Duke Cosimo II de' Medici. When he enlarged the Palace he turned the front rooms over to this purpose and ordered Pietro da Cortona, the great Baroque muralist, to decorate the ceilings. The frescoes by Pietro da Cortona and other ceiling painters who followed have, by their subjects, given names to the various gallery rooms—the Iliad Room, the Room of Jupiter, of Mars, of Apollo, of Venus, and so forth.

The sister museum of the Pitti—the Uffizi Gallery across the river in Florence (of which I have the honor also to be administrator)—is arranged in the modern manner, with quiet backgrounds and soft lighting. The collections of both these institutions owe their size, quality, and very existence to the passion for art and art collecting by the Medici over the centuries. The Uffizi, roughly, was the official state art collection, as gathered by the Medici. The Pitti was the personal Medici family collection housed with

COSIMO I DE' MEDICI AND ELEONORA OF
TOLEDO AND THEIR CHILDREN
by Giovanni Antonio de' Rossi
Italian, 1517-1575

the family living quarters. Both collections were left to the people of Florence in 1737, at the death of the last of the Medici, and have been public since then.

The Pitti includes some medieval pictures, as well as wonderful Flemish and Spanish works. However, the strength of this gallery lies in Italian Renaissance and Baroque paintings; and our tour will show us mostly these. The Baroque is the seventeenth-century style that followed the Renaissance.

In Renaissance art the human race appeared serene, cool, and unperturbed. Painting, sculpture, and architecture all were generally composed of straight lines or simple, refined curves; there were no sudden thrusts or shifts, and the surfaces of the pictures—and the buildings—were without deep penetration or restlessness. But in Baroque this is all changed. Mankind seems troubled, brooding—and burdened by responsibility. Paintings and buildings are marked by extravagant twisted shapes, and light is used to create a disturbing drama of mysterious shadows and flashing highlights; the straight or arched line of the Renaissance is replaced by the spiral or interrupted line, and the serene calm yields to a powerful restlessness which is nevertheless majestic in its flourishes. The Baroque art of movement, drama, and, above all, light, links the Renaissance with modern times, so that the end of our tour will bring us to the threshold of our own day.

We enter the Pitti by the Gate of Bacchus and come to the first of a long series of rooms running along the front of the Palace.

AND NOW YOUR
COLORSLIDE TOUR BEGINS—

We stop first before this round panel, or "tondo," of the *Madonna and Child*, painted by Fra Filippo Lippi in 1452 and, accordingly, belonging to the early Renaissance. Not long before, in the late Middle Ages, an artist would have given us a vision of heaven with the Madonna enthroned in majesty; mother and Child would have been imposing and more than human in scale. But the heavenly figures in this picture are down to earth; they are human and natural. We are seeing the new spirit of the Renaissance, its humanism and realism. The dignified Madonna is physically beautiful. The Child plays with a pomegranate, from which He has plucked a seed. The artist's joy in the tiniest realistic detail is shown in every square inch of the panel. The background scenes are episodes in the Virgin's life, but Fra Filippo has depicted them as scenes from the everyday life of his time. By seeming to exist convincingly in deep space constructed according to the laws of perspective, these scenes tell us that art was turning to nature and this world, dealing with things as they are—rather than presenting symbolic images.

1. Madonna and Child with Scenes from the Life of the Virgin

by FRA FILIPPO LIPPI (Florentine, about 1406-1469)

In the Room of Saturn we now see a panel of St. Mary Magdalene executed by Perugino (*peh-roo-*JEE-*noh*) between 1496 and 1500—half a century later than Fra Filippo Lippi's fine circular painting. At first glance the figure of the Magdalene may seem very like Fra Filippo's figure of the Madonna. However, there are significant differences—for example, Fra Filippo surrounded his central Madonna with many figures and much narrative action, all worked out in minute detail. See how Perugino suppressed detail—except in the face, neck, and hands—and how he made the entire background a single area of dark tone. This emphasis on simplicity is characteristic of the later period, and so is the fact that Perugino did not give the Magdalene the features of a particular person. He generalized. He was concerned with ideal form, with painting sacred personages as he imagined the noblest and most graceful human beings might appear. The stateliness and intense spiritual feeling of this picture we shall see again—for Perugino, at his very best, reminds us of the early art of his most celebrated pupil, Raphael.

2. *Mary Magdalene*

by PERUGINO (Central Italian, about 1445-1523)

3. *The Deposition*

by FRA BARTOLOMMEO (Florentine, 1474-1517)

In the Room of Jupiter we see Fra Bartolommeo's (*frah bar-toh-lahm-MAY-oh's*) *Deposition*, or Descent from the Cross, painted about a year before the artist's death. Here, the most tragic of all subjects is handled with the noble simplicity and quiet grandeur of the classical phase of the High Renaissance. Fra Bartolommeo, who was a man of religion as well as an artist, tried to show us a moment full of the most intense drama, but nevertheless a moment of dignity and restraint. A grief beyond description is stamped on St. John's face, and on the Madonna's even more, but neither gives way to uncontrolled emotion. No one moves physically, not even St. Mary Magdalene, who has thrown herself across Christ's feet; the only outward movement that we see is in the drapery of the saints to the left and right. Here, the agitated swirls give us a clue to the inner feelings of the actors of this drama. The four figures in this early sixteenth-century painting are brought into one majestic structure through their idealized forms, spiritually bound together by the grief of the occasion and, compositionally, by their harmonious contours.

4. *Portrait of a Goldsmith*

by RIDOLFO DEL GHIRLANDAIO

(Florentine, 1483-1561)

SLIDE 4

In the Saturn Room hangs this *Portrait of a Goldsmith* by Ridolfo del Ghirlandaio (*ree-*DAWL*-foh dell gear-lan-*DAH*-yoh*), painted around 1500. As you already know, the collection was originally the private possession of Grand Dukes of the Medici family, who collected portraits of their royal relatives and important persons the way you and I save photographs of people who are important to us. To make sure that they would have the portraits they wanted, they hired painters to be in constant attendance at their court. For this reason, the Pitti is rich in portraits, and we shall see many of them on our tour. This example is not an official portrait painted for the grand-ducal court, but a typical fine portrait of the early sixteenth century in Florence. It was once thought to be by Leonardo da Vinci, and does show elements of the great painter's style: we see the subject half-length and in three-quarter view, looking as though he were at an open window, high above a distant landscape. The figure is very precisely drawn, but the landscape is light, misty, and atmospheric. The goldsmith's hair is worn long, and he examines a jewel that he holds in his right hand.

Here is another work of the classical period of the Italian Renaissance, an altarpiece executed for a monastery in 1518 by Andrea del Sarto, whom the poet Browning called the "perfect painter." When we look at this altarpiece we must imagine ourselves to be worshipers in a church—men of religion, too, able to appreciate fine points in doctrine. We see four saints in a heated discussion. Notice how this artist used his skill at representing gesture and movement to make these figures develop a message and drive it home. St. Lawrence, with the grill on which he was roasted, holds a book ready, while St. Peter Martyr holds his book as if to say, "Look, it says so right here." St. Francis points to himself as if to say, "And in my opinion . . ." And St. Augustine grasps his crozier in one hand and makes a challenging gesture with the other, as though losing his patience with St. Peter Martyr. St. Sebastian and St. Mary Magdalene are not engaged in the discussion; perhaps, as they kneel, they have seen the heavenly vision of God the Father holding the crucified Christ, which is painted at the top of the picture. Andrea is saying, then, that the Trinity endures forever, no matter how its most eminent worshipers may disagree about it.

5. *The Dispute on the Holy Trinity*

by ANDREA DEL SARTO

(Florentine, 1486-1531)

Vasari, the biographer of Italian Renaissance artists, says of Agnolo Doni (AH-*nyoh-loh* DAW-*nee*)—whose portrait painted by Raphael (RAF-*ay-ell*) in Florence, in 1506, is in the Saturn Room—that he was "averse to spending money for other things, but for paintings and sculptures, in which he greatly delighted, he would willingly pay, although he still did so as frugally as possible." This dignified, sober portrait of the classical period of the Renaissance reveals these qualities, for Raphael painted it with high finish and painstaking realism. The distant landscape and sky of the background, in contrast with the reds, yellows, and browns of figure and foreground, are soft blues and greens, and are completely flooded with a marvelous light. By this means, Raphael achieved a soft, atmospheric effect that emphasizes the solidity of the portrait figure in the foreground and gives the whole picture great depth. Raphael is one of the towering geniuses of art; and few portraits in history have achieved such an effect of harmony, poise, and simple grandeur, of the nobility of the human presence.

6. *Portrait of Agnolo Doni*

by RAPHAEL (Central Italian, 1483-1520)

7. *La Gravida*

by RAPHAEL

(Central Italian, 1483-1520)

The Pitti owns another portrait that the young Raphael painted in Florence within a year of his *Agnolo Doni*—a portrait of a woman in red, black, and dull gold. During his Florentine years, the artist was strongly influenced by Florentine painters, especially by Leonardo da Vinci. The landscape background of the portrait of Doni, for example, could almost have been painted by Leonardo himself. There is no landscape background in *La Gravida* (*lah* GRAH-*vee-dah*)—which means "the pregnant woman"—but we may sense echoes of Leonardo's *Mona Lisa* in the figure. The painting, like Raphael's other portraits, is a masterpiece of spiritual balance; the artist saw, even in such a subject, an opportunity to create an image of serenity and poise. The woman is dignified—a commanding presence—and all elements of the painting are in complete harmony with one another. Raphael did not tolerate distracting details, but rendered form solidly, simply, with boldness and breadth. The classicism of his mature, High Renaissance style in Rome was already developed before he left Florence for Rome in 1508.

The *Madonna of the Chair* is one of the most famous of Raphael's Madonnas and one of the best loved pictures in the world. See how much more there is here than a celebration of motherhood or an easily grasped ideal of human beauty. These figures are organized magnificently within the circular panel. The curves of the panel itself are repeated, again and again, in the rounded forms of the heads and arms and details of the post. They are repeated in the space of the picture, too: note how this rounding makes the Madonna's right arm come forward, and how the infant St. John the Baptist, on the right, is put into the depth of the picture. Although the figures combine to make a beautiful flat pattern on the surface of the panel, they also make a magnificent arrangement in space, for the forms are rounded, like sculpture. The color is clear and brilliant, and there are no superfluous details. This painting was executed in 1516 in Rome, when Raphael was at the height of his powers. Although still a young man he was hailed as the "Prince of Painters," and became both a popular hero and a high papal official.

8. *Madonna of the Chair*

by RAPHAEL (Central Italian, 1483-1520)

9. *La Donna Velata*

by RAPHAEL (Central Italian, 1483-1520)

Our last painting by the Prince of Painters is a famous portrait—*La Donna Velata*, the Lady with a Veil. In his portraits of women Raphael usually idealized the sitter, as he did here. This lady has individual character, however, in spite of the perfection of her features and the pure oval of her face. And, in spite of the serenity and poise of Raphael's classical vision, there is no other portrait, perhaps, in which we find him conveying such physical warmth and sensuous vitality. This versatile master rivaled the Venetians Giorgione (*jor-*JOE*-neh*) and Titian (TISH-*un*) at their own game! Even the clothing is alive—see the frothy, rippling curves in the sleeve, which is so richly colored and painted with so delicate a touch. There is just a suggestion of mystery in the way that the figure emerges from the dark mass of the background. Through this sureness of touch, and through the ease with which the conception was developed and realized, we know that we are looking at the work of a mature artist of tremendous ability, at the peak of his creative power.

SLIDE 10

We come now to a great portrait of a youthful Italian prince. We can see here why Bronzino (*brun*-ZEE-*noh*), who was a most polished and urbane portraitist, became the official painter of the court of Cosimo I de' Medici, Duke of Florence and, later, Grand Duke of Tuscany. This portrait of another Renaissance prince, Guidobaldo della Rovere (*gwee-do*-BAL-*doh del-la* RO-*veh-reh*), Duke of Urbino, shows us that the artist spared no effort to make his sitter as imposing and splendid as possible. Guidobaldo stands like a statue and stares boldly out of the picture. The figure is shown three-quarter length, a proportion preferred to half-length in the mid-sixteenth century because it was more impressive. The painter's brush has dwelt lovingly upon the details of the sumptuous fabrics and intricate, costly armor. See how the hand resting on the dog's head has been exaggerated, making the fingers appear longer and more aristocratic than in nature. Because Bronzino made his sitters appear so distinguished, so commanding, his style became an accepted model for formal court portraiture all over Europe.

SLIDE 11

This painting in the Room of Castagnoli is one side of a large standard, or banner, that Sodoma (SUH-*duh-mah*) painted in 1525 for the Company of St. Sebastian in Siena, to be carried in processions. Sodoma's aim was to reproduce the ideally beautiful image of the human figure that was developed by Raphael, whose form and grace are shown in Sodoma's figure of the Saint, and by Leonardo, of whom we are reminded by the facial type and the strong contrasts of light and shade. We see the same influences again in the landscape, whose blue distances are flooded with light and air. In its dreamy, imaginative quality it reminds us of the ideal landscape we saw earlier in Raphael's *Portrait of Agnolo Doni*. But we should not think that Sodoma had no qualities of his own. To the forms learned from the supreme masters he added his own powerful sense of drama. The Saint swings his body as the arrows pierce his flesh, and an angel radiating shafts of light swoops down from heaven with a martyr's crown. The harsh and twisted shape of the tree balances the figure with a movement in the opposite direction, and adds to the emotional agitation of the scene.

10. *Portrait of Guidobaldo della Rovere*

by BRONZINO

(Florentine, 1502-1572)

11. *St. Sebastian*

by SODOMA

(North Italian, 1477-1549)

12. The Three Ages of Man

by GIORGIONE (Venetian, about 1478-1510)

SLIDE 12

The number of unquestioned works by the Venetian painter Giorgione, a short-lived sixteenth-century artist of supreme genius, can be counted on the fingers of one hand. This famous panel in the Room of Jupiter shows his poetic vision. We do not really know what he painted here, in spite of the intriguing title, but the message of harmony and concord is unmistakable. The boy in the center and the young man on his left are not shown to us as individuals, but as ideally handsome types, simply but beautifully clothed. A golden radiance of light plays across the faces; it softens and adds even greater richness to the deep, harmonious Venetian color of the garments. This light is reflected back into the shadows which, accordingly, become transparent and allow us to see features instead of hiding them. The relationship of the figures is very interesting. The boy is looking at the sheet of music that he holds in his hands. The young man turns toward the boy and points toward the music. The old man in the foreground, by looking out toward us, establishes a connection with us, the spectators, and so involves us somehow in the action of the picture.

In the Room of Flora we stop before a painting in which magnificent color and majestic arrangement are combined with a story of terrible suffering. It should become clear to us that a great painting is not necessarily a beautiful picture. This *Martyrdom of St. Agatha* was painted in Rome in 1520, by Sebastiano del Piombo (*say-bas-*TYAH*-noh* dell PYOM-*boh*), who signed the picture "Sebastianus the Venetian." The Saint has steeled herself against the ordeal. The soldiers in the background seem to suffer with her, and the Roman praetor at the left, who has ordered this torture, is incredulous as he sees that Agatha will submit to it rather than deny her Christian faith. The Saint's white body is contrasted with the swarthy faces of the men; such a contrast helps to heighten the drama and St. Agatha becomes the outstanding visual element, just as she is the most important figure in the story that is being told. The light playing on the rich yellow, blue, and orange garments of the praetor makes him the secondary center of our interest, even though the artist has daringly placed him at the extreme edge of the picture.

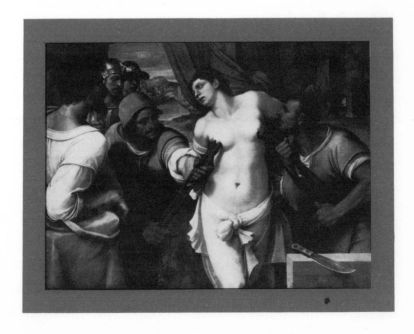

13. *The Martyrdom of St. Agatha*

by SEBASTIANO DEL PIOMBO (Venetian, about 1485-1547)

14. The Concert

by TITIAN (Venetian, about 1490-1576)

This *Concert*, by Titian (TISH-*un*), hangs in the Room of Venus. It was thought to be by Giorgione when Cardinal Leopoldo de' Medici acquired it three hundred years ago, and it certainly reminds us of Giorgione's *Three Ages of Man*, which we saw earlier. Both pictures are visual poetry and both have a golden richness of color; both have musical subjects, and show three half-length figures, of whom one is a boy, one a young man, and one an older man. Perhaps Venetian artists chose such themes because of their interest in subtle differences of facial coloring, skin texture, and bone structure in people of different ages. The painting by Titian, however, seems less dreamlike; to Giorgione's poetry, Titian added a stronger sense of psychology and of the real world. The monk playing the clavichord at the left is one of the most fascinating figures in all Italian art. Especially remarkable is the suggestion of the oneness of the musician and his music. The hands—such hands!—are charged with expression, and though the eyes gaze into the distance, it is an inward vision that they see.

We do not know the subject of this portrait by Titian, although it was once believed to be an Englishman, the Duke of Norfolk. Just the same, we know a great deal about his character, because the artist tells us through his art. Titian was a master of psychological portraiture. In the sixteenth century artists had fully mastered painting techniques, and were no longer interested in realism and detail just because they wanted to see how far they could go. Now they simplified and concentrated. Titian needed to do little more than suggest a few details here and there in order to create an illusion of a sumptuous costume. The tunic is just a dark mass of tone against a dark background—with hints of significant details: touches of lace at the sleeves, gloves in the subject's right hand, a few strokes to indicate a gold chain around his neck. Our attention is focused on the head, where the color glows —and on the hands. The face is dreamy and mysterious, but the dark eyes fix us squarely. Every part of this canvas contributes to the perfection of this portrait, one of the finest in all art.

15. Portrait of a Man

by TITIAN

(Venetian, about 1490-1576)

This *Mary Magdalene* in the Apollo Room was painted by Titian for the Duke of Urbino between 1530 and 1540. In the lower left-hand corner of the picture we see a little ointment jar, an emblem of the Magdalene, like her long, golden hair. The Saint is shown in penitence for her life of sin before she met Christ, and her raised eyes are swollen with weeping. The golden luster of her flesh and the darker gold of her hair are set off by a dark landscape background and a corner of blue sky torn by clouds. The rendering of texture in the hair shows the artist's extraordinary technical skill, and is characteristically Venetian. The Venetian painters were the first to try to render sense impressions in paint—and to paint the actual world as we see and feel it in its human significance, rather than according to the intellect alone. We might even say that Titian invented painting as we understand the word today, and that, by comparison, all painting before him was colored drawing.

16. *Mary Magdalene*

by TITIAN (Venetian, about 1490-1576)

17. *La Bella*

by TITIAN (Venetian, about 1490-1576)

SLIDE 17

Here is another great portrait by Titian, done around 1536 or 1537. It is less remarkable for the beauty of the face—which accounts for its traditional name *La Bella*—than for its perfect harmony and peace. The sitter's luxurious brocade dress gave the artist a chance to create a color symphony of deep reds, rich blues, gold, warm flesh, jewelry, and pearls. The contours of the ample forms are soft and rounded; and La Bella herself is composed, serene, self-confident. Quietly, she allows the drama of color and texture to take the center of the stage. Raphael's *Portrait of Agnolo Doni*, we recall, was half-length, a treatment characteristic of the beginning of the sixteenth century that gave way to three-quarter-length portraiture in the middle of the century. Now the figure fills and dominates the picture space. These developments were in keeping with the tendency of the times toward greater enrichment and display—another means of enabling Titian to impress the spectator with his sitter's regality and splendor.

At one time it was believed that Giorgione painted this little picture, which is not far away from Titian's *Portrait of a Man*. It is easy enough to see why: the deep Venetian color; the ample Venetian type of feminine beauty; the composition with two half-length figures; the gems and golden chain resting upon warm flesh; the contrast of fair and dark skin, of skin and hair, of skin and fur—we could go on and on. We are already familiar with these qualities in Giorgione and in the early Titian; and Titian was their source in Dossi's art. However, we can see a major difference between Dossi on the one hand, and Giorgione and the early Titian on the other. In their pictures of around 1500 Giorgione and Titian built serene, poetic dream worlds. There is poetry in this picture, too, but we would be amazed if we found in Giorgione and Titian the bestiality of this leering satyr with bared teeth.

18. *Nymph Pursued by a Satyr*

by DOSSO DOSSI (North Italian, about 1479-1542)

19. Portrait of a Woman

by BORDONE (Venetian, 1500-1571)

Hanging above Giorgione's *Three Ages of Man* is another Venetian painting done about twenty-five years later. This was once called the "Nurse of the Medici," but it more likely represents a woman of a noble family. Her dress is rich, especially the red bodice ending in lace shoulders and collar. Bordone (*bore-*DOH-*neh*) was a pupil of Titian, of whose art we are reminded by the golden light, the fresh-looking flesh tints of the face, and the gleaming russet—or "Titian"—hair. Venetian painters of the Renaissance loved to paint what meets the eye. They were not interested in trivial or accidental details—they suppressed them and painted with great breadth and rich deep tones. Detail and structure, as we have seen, were often suggested rather than worked out completely. The light that bathes their pictures picked out significant details here and there—the faces, the hands, and enough of the costume to tell us what the whole is like. In such art the paint surface of which the image is composed seems itself to become a kind of rare, precious substance, adding another quality, as it were, for the observer to grasp and enjoy.

The large *Patience* hanging on the right-hand wall of the Room of Prometheus was painted by Salviati (*sahl*-VYAH-*tee*), and is a typical Florentine work of the mid-sixteenth century. The new currents in art at this time came from Venice, where artists were interested in light, in color, in loose brushwork, in painting as a spontaneous expression of joy in life. Florentine painters did not wish to break new ground, and remained faithful to the classical, linear tradition of Raphael and Michelangelo. Their forms were solid, like sculpture, with smooth modeling, and they tended to be studied and elegant, developing their classical subject matter in a learned, scholarly way, with many literary and scientific references. Here we have an elaborate allegory, for the figure of Patience is not that of a human being who has been imprisoned, but an abstract quality personified. We see her as an almost nude classical goddess with an elaborate coiffure; her left ankle is daintily chained to the wall, and alongside her head is an armillary sphere—a working model of the motions of the planets. Much of the symbolic meaning is lost to us.

20. *Patience*

by SALVIATI (Florentine, 1510-1563)

21. *Portrait of Vincenzo Zeno*

by TINTORETTO (Venetian, 1518-1594)

SLIDE 21

Here is a great portrait by the great Tintoretto (*tin-toe-*RET-*toh*)—for Renaissance Venice was full of tremendous painting talents in the sixteenth century. Even when their subjects were religious, these men were inclined to dwell upon the joy of life in opulent Venice, and to suggest a rich life of the senses. Musical subjects, as we have seen, recur in their paintings; our sense of touch is evoked through their concern with textures of hair, fur, flesh, silk, velvet, jewels, and brocade. In this marvelous portrait of another of those wonderful old Venetian noblemen, we see these qualities once again —here combined with a smoldering sunset landscape beyond the open window. A rosy light is cast over the entire picture space. About Vincenzo Zeno (*vin-*CHEN-*tso* TSAY-*no*) himself we know nothing except, as the inscription tells us, that he was 74 when Tintoretto captured his vigorous features on canvas.

22. *Portrait of Daniele Barbaro*

by VERONESE (Venetian, 1528-1588)

Daniele Barbaro, the possible subject of this portrait by Veronese (*vay-roe-*NAY-*seh*), was the Venetian ambassador to the English court of Edward VI. In addition, he wrote a book on perspective and translated the Latin author Vitruvius' *Ten Books on Architecture*. To the painting of Barbaro's likeness Veronese brought the ability to show dignity and strength of character as much through mood and setting as through observation of the sensitive face and hands. The portrait is three-quarter length, painted in broad masses of tone, and shows the Venetian love of textures of fur and cloth. Barbaro is dressed in black velvet, and a silvery light comes from the open window on our right, falling upon his ermine cloak and long silver-streaked black beard. His right arm rests on a column base; his left hand holds a small object wrapped in cloth. At first glance, this portrait may look like almost any other by the great Venetians of the sixteenth century, but Veronese had a remarkable decorative sense, and his paintings inevitably became rich feasts for the eyes.

In the Room of Justice we see Veronese's large *Baptism of Christ*, painted around 1575 and showing the full majesty of his mature style. We can see that, originally, this painting was planned to hang high on a wall: the perspective is constructed so that we see everything as though we were below this scene and looking upward. Again there is a grand patterning of picture surface—a magnificent piece of decoration. The idealized and classical figures, radiant with light, have been wonderfully painted with broad strokes of the brush; and the contrast between the massed dark and light tones is extremely dramatic. The foreground of the picture is dark, and only the great tree, the head of Jesus, and the baptismal cup are silhouetted against the bright sky. In a straight line with Jesus and the water of the baptism we see the dove of the Holy Ghost—the source of all the light that falls on the figures. Jesus kneels in the river Jordan as an angel holds His garment, and St. John the Baptist, dressed in fur, pours the water.

23. *Baptism of Christ*

by VERONESE

(Venetian, 1528-1588)

From the doorway of the Room of the Education of Jupiter, near the entrance, we see a painting that marks an abrupt contrast with everything that we have seen so far. It is a characteristic example by Caravaggio (*ka-ra-*VAHD-*joh*), Italy's great painter of the seventeenth century, who executed it in the year 1608. Although the subject is taken from ancient mythology, the artist evidently tried to be as unclassical as he possibly could— he even made fun of the classical vision of perfection and harmony. The light-and-shade is so violent in its contrasts that only the body and wing details emerge from the darkness. With Caravaggio, the dark shadow areas often become the most important shapes in the picture, a style that immediately had tremendous influence on European painting. Cupid is an urchin from the streets, sleeping heavily, with his mouth open and his limbs twisted. Caravaggio made him deliberately ungraceful. This kind of realism goes far beyond merely creating an illusion of something solid and convincing behind the frame of the picture. Caravaggio had a violent need to cut through the idealistic tradition of the Renaissance and show us the world without glossing over any of its weaknesses and faults. There is no serenity in his vision.

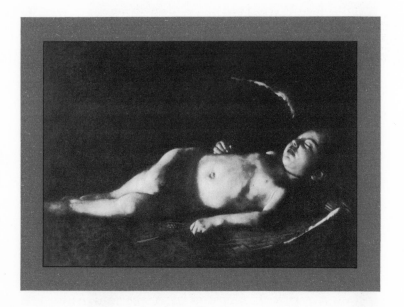

24. *Sleeping Cupid*

by CARAVAGGIO (North Italian, 1573-1610)

25. *Cleopatra*

by RENI (North Italian, 1575-1642)

Guido Reni's (GWEE-*do* RAY-*nee's*) *Cleopatra*, which is in the Music Room, was painted early in the seventeenth century. It does not remind us of the contemporaneous work of Caravaggio, but of earlier paintings—specifically, of the Renaissance. See how closely Reni repeated the pose and expression that we saw in Sodoma's *St. Sebastian*. This echo is probably no accident, even though Reni worked a hundred years later. Reni and Sodoma both studied the forms of the leading painters of the High Renaissance—Reni because he belonged to the so-called Eclectic school of artists in Bologna, who worshiped the classical style of the earlier sixteenth century. The Eclectics borrowed, as the name suggests. As they put it, they tried to combine "the composition of Raphael, the drawing of Michelangelo, and the coloring of Titian." In this picture Cleopatra is shown committing suicide by putting a poisonous asp to her bosom after she and Antony were defeated in battle and Antony took his own life. The story is handled with far more melodrama than it would have received a century before, but the color harmony enchants us with its tones of silver, faded lavender, and pale gold.

This *Judith* by Allori (*ahl*-LAW-*ree*) and Caravaggio's *Sleeping Cupid* in the Room of the Education of Jupiter were painted around the same time, and both pictures reveal the use of the bold, spotlight effect of illumination invented by Caravaggio. But the resemblance ends there—for Caravaggio was a realist and loved nature plain and unadorned. Allori, obviously, was a classicist, and felt that nature needed to be refined and elevated before it was fit to be seen in a painting. He used Caravaggio's violent light-and-shade only for its drama; his true interest was in brilliant, dazzling color, gorgeous textiles, physically beautiful models, and elegant drawing. No other severed head has ever been carried with such aristocracy. It happens often in the history of art that the big ideas of great innovators are ignored by their most charming successors, who nevertheless make successful use of the new forms in their efforts to please the taste of the patrons of art. In this way, revolutionary contributions are made part of established tradition, and are popularized.

26. *Judith*

by CRISTOFANO ALLORI

(Florentine, 1577-1621)

27. *Portrait of Justus Lipsius and His Pupils*

by RUBENS (Flemish, 1577-1640)

In the Room of Mars we see a portrait of four men by Rubens. The artist himself is in this portrait and we see him standing at the left; next to him is his younger brother Philip, who holds a pen. The other two persons are Lipsius, the great legal scholar, and John Wouverius. This group of eminent Flemings came together in Italy in 1602. Through the language of art, they are being compared to Seneca, the Roman philosopher, of whom we see a bust in the wall niche, where a vase of tulips has been placed as a mark of respect. More than any other seventeenth-century painter, Rubens, although Flemish, carried on the Venetian tradition. Here we have an astounding display of skillful paint handling, brilliant contrasts of color and light, and glowing freshness. The alert bearing of the figures, the vitality of their expressions, the dramatic composition, the elaborate setting, and the shimmering landscape background are characteristic of the bold, fluid painting style of this century which we call Baroque.

28. *Allegory of War*

by RUBENS (Flemish, 1577-1640)

Nearby is one of Rubens' last works, painted for the artist Sustermans in 1638. We will soon see a picture by Sustermans, who was court painter to the Medici and left this picture to the family in his will. Here we have an astounding picture. In the tremendous rush and leaping energy we see Baroque painting at the height of its vitality. In the center is the armor-clad war god, Mars; his shield is on his left arm, his sword in his right hand. At right, screaming Fury waves a torch and drags him away from the nude figure of Venus, who tries to hold him back. Mars tramples on a book, as three figures in the right lower corner are hurled to the ground. They are Charity, who holds a baby close; Concord, her arm around a lute; and the Arts, a prone male figure who holds high a pair of dividers, symbol of skill and intellect. At the left, next to the distracted figure of Government, we see the Classical Roman Temple of Janus. The door of this temple was closed in time of peace and open in time of war. The Thirty Years War was raging in 1638 and we can see here an allegorical reference to it. The Baroque period loved to express its ideas in elaborate allegories and pageants.

The Pitti is rich in masterworks by Rubens. A diplomat as well as a painter, the great Flemish master of the Baroque for the most part created huge historical paintings, altarpieces, and official courtly portraits. He needed many assistants to help him with these projects. But when he retired to spend his last years with his young wife he made pictures which show a new poetic vision—they are hymns to nature and to the joy of life. They were painted entirely by the artist's own hand and reveal his deepest personal feelings. In this landscape, on the wall opposite the preceding picture, the curving road takes our eyes deep into the extended space of the Belgian plain. So do the gold- and red-tinted clouds of the late afternoon sky. An extraordinary light plays over the scene, making the entire picture vibrant and alive with nervous vitality in every small detail. Rarely in the history of world art do we find such an outpouring of new creative energy toward the close of an artistic career.

29. *Peasants Returning from the Fields*

by RUBENS (Flemish, 1577-1640)

Guido Bentivoglio (GWEE-*do ben-tee*-VOLE-*yo*), whose portrait we see here, was a diplomat for the Vatican, and became a cardinal in 1621. This elegant portrait, done shortly after, shows him in his new red robes. Van Dyck (*van* DIKE) was a pupil and friend of Rubens and is similar in his skilled, flowing brushwork and rich color and light. His portraits have great vigor, but he had no wish to endow his sitters with the tremendous animal energy that we almost always find in portraits by Rubens. Instead, he emphasized their inner control, aristocratic bearing, and qualities of personal distinction. Here we see one of the artist's finest works, painted when he was only twenty-two. It is simple in conception and executed with great ease and naturalness. Van Dyck was so successful in aristocratic portraiture that Charles I of England appointed him painter to the king and made him a knight—Sir Anthony Van Dyck. The style of painting that we see here became the basis for a tradition in English and American portraiture that persists to this day.

30. Portrait of Cardinal Guido Bentivoglio

by VAN DYCK (Flemish, 1599-1641)

31. Portrait of Prince Christian of Denmark

by SUSTERMANS (Flemish, 1597-1681)

This charming *Portrait of Prince Christian of Denmark* was painted by Sustermans around 1662 and hangs in the Iliad Room. The youth was then about sixteen. He is shown in armor, with a silken sash across his chest and an elaborate lace collar around his neck. This is one of the most famous of Sustermans' portraits and, because it is so spontaneous, one of the most unusual. The handsome boy's heavy eyes give him a dreamy, thoughtful expression that contrasts with his luxurious clothing and armor. The pose is simple rather than courtly and self-conscious. Every detail of hair, armor, and lace collar is painted with the utmost accuracy and care. Sustermans painted almost nothing but portraits, which he did according to his native Flemish tradition, although he was official painter to the Medici court in Florence for forty years. However, in the seventeenth century, national differences in style were less pronounced than previously and, to a great extent, there was a common European style. Here then we have a fine example of Europe's aristocratic portraiture in the later seventeenth century.

32. *Madonna and Child*

by MURILLO (Spanish, 1617-1682)

Our last picture of this tour of the Pitti is a famous *Madonna and Child*. Critics of art have always admired the lovely, creamy light in paintings by the Spanish master Murillo (*moo*-REE-*lyoh*), and it is true that this light gives his paintings an airy and transparent effect unsurpassed in the seventeenth century. However, that is not why this Madonna has been so popular with visitors to the Pitti for three centuries. Murillo spoke directly from the heart. He did not paint for aristocrats and intellectuals. Poor as a boy, and self-taught, he saw and painted with the simple, unaffected sentiment of the common people to whom he always belonged. What Murillo had to say to us requires no interpretation. The Madonna and the Child both have extraordinary grace and charm. The artist did not try to produce an impression of the religious grandeur of the Queen of Heaven, but the impression of motherhood in its most natural and spontaneous form.

Our tour now ends. I hope that it has contributed to your understanding and pleasure, and that some day you can come in person to the incomparably beautiful medieval city of Florence, so that we can welcome you to the glorious Pitti itself. I would like you to see the originals of the choice masterpieces that have appeared on the screen as well as this historic palace and treasure house, which has so magnificent a setting in the park of the Boboli Gardens, overlooking the birthplace of the art and science of the modern world.

Filippo Rossi